T0190747

ORDINARY
PEOPLE
CHANGE
— THE —
WORLD

I am Stephen Hawking

BRAD MELTZER

illustrated by **Christopher Eliopoulos**

 ROCKY POND BOOKS

I am **STEPHEN HAWKING.**

Do you know what a boundary is?
It's something that tells you the limit, how far you can go.
But nothing can limit our minds.

Today, people call me one of the smartest thinkers of all time, but on my first day at preschool, I cried non-stop because I missed my parents so much.

Growing up in northern London, I wasn't the best student.

My work was messy and my handwriting wasn't very good.

WHY DO I NEED GOOD HANDWRITING?

THOSE ARE THE RULES—DON'T ASK QUESTIONS.

I didn't always use a wheelchair. You'll hear that story soon.

Back when I could walk and run, I wasn't great at sports.

When it came to choosing teams, I was almost always picked last.

I GUESS WE'RE STUCK WITH HAWKING.

When I was twelve years old, a schoolmate made a bet that I would never be successful.

I'LL BET YOU A BAG OF CANDY ON IT.

YOU GOT IT.

Sometimes it can be hard when you're different.
But I liked seeing things in my own way, a more creative way.
When my dad built a doll house for my sister, I added plumbing and lighting.

I was also very curious, taking apart my toy trains to see how they worked.

I wasn't so good at putting them back together.

Thankfully, my parents encouraged my curiosity.

In our house, we did a lot of what you're doing right now: reading books.

Our house was full of them—on shelves, on the furniture . . . everywhere.

Since we had almost no heating, the walls of books helped keep out the cold.

If you came over to my house for a playdate, sometimes my family would even read during dinner.

Other times, my parents would have us debate topics that weren't usually discussed by kids.

People called us eccentric, which is a nice way of saying we were weird. But I liked having my mind constantly challenged.

My father's job was studying tropical diseases.
He'd let me look through the microscopes at his lab...

He'd even show me around the insect house, where he kept infected mosquitoes.

But the best gift my parents gave me was nurturing my sense of wonder.
We'd lie on the grass, staring up at the sky.

The stars called to me.
What was beyond called to me.

My parents taught me to question things and think big.
They taught me to use research and science to find answers

The human mind is incredible.

It can imagine the beauty of the heavens or the tiny particles we're made of.

But to achieve our full potential, we all need a spark.

So often, it comes from a teacher.

Mr. Tahta opened my eyes to the power of math.

Behind every exceptional person is an exceptional teacher.

In high school, my sense of wonder grew.
My friends and I would invent games and build computers together.

Best of all, we'd have long conversations about whatever we found interesting, from radio-controlled cars to one of my favorite topics.

To find the answer, I needed to understand something called physics, which is the study of matter and energy and how they work in time and space.

I started college when I was seventeen.

I didn't have many friends, so I joined the Boat Club to meet people.

Since I was the smallest, my job was to steer and tell everyone when to row.

But in my first race, I accidentally sent the boat off course and got us disqualified.

WHAT'D YOU DO?

YOU MESSED IT UP!

Here's my real secret: Back then, I wasn't always interested in my schoolwork. I cared more about going to parties.

Soon enough, though, life was about to take an unexpected turn.

In my last year of college, I fell down some stairs, thinking I was clumsy.

At first, the doctor made a joke of it.

STOP PARTYING SO MUCH.

My body was getting harder to control.

At twenty years old, I didn't want anyone to worry, so I kept my fears to myself.

At Christmas, I fell while ice-skating and couldn't get up.

My mother knew something was wrong.

After many tests, I got terrible news.
I had a rare disease called ALS—amyotrophic lateral sclerosis—which affects the nerve cells until the muscles in your body don't work anymore.

They told me I had two and a half years to live.

I was twenty-one years old.
I was scared and in shock.
But when they told me my life would end, it made me realize how much more I wanted to accomplish.
Right then, every new day became a bonus.

With life, I had hope.
My disease was breaking my body.
Eventually, it would slur my speech and then take my voice entirely.
But the one thing it could never touch?
My brain.

One of my biggest eureka moments came while I was getting into bed. I had to go very slowly because of my disability, which meant I had more time to think.

A black hole is an area in outer space with gravity that's so powerful, nothing can escape its pull.

On that night, I came up with a new theory—that the boundary of a black hole can never decrease, never get smaller.

I was rewriting the rules for how we understand black holes.

Eventually, that led to an even bigger question.
Could anything escape the pull of a black hole?
To my surprise, the answer was yes.

IT'S TRUE! EVEN AT THE BOUNDRY, WHERE IT PULLS HARDEST,

A CERTAIN TYPE OF ENERGY CAN ESCAPE.

Today, that energy is called "Hawking radiation."
It's one of my greatest discoveries.
It also helped me prove that instead of always expanding, black holes could shrink, evaporate, and even vanish.

TH-THAT'S NOT POSSIBLE.

IT IS. I HAD IT WRONG BEFORE.

OH MY.

To prove my new theory, I had to rethink and modify my first theory.

THAT'S NOT A BAD THING.

THE BEST SCIENTISTS ALWAYS KEEP ASKING QUESTIONS.

REAL INTELLIGENCE MEANS YOU'RE WILLING TO ADMIT YOU MAY BE WRONG.

In the end, it became clear that black holes weren't completely black. And they certainly weren't inescapable.

In life, as in outer space, even for the darkest holes, there's always a way out.

All you need is the right energy.

Over time, my discoveries revolutionized astrophysics.
But as my disease got worse, I lost the use of my hands.
I couldn't write or type, so for people to understand my ideas,
I needed help from others, like my wife, Jane.

My disease took so much from me,
but it also gave me skills no one else had,
helping me use my creativity to solve problems
no one else could.

Eventually, I realized that the universe has no boundaries—
just like the human mind.

In my early thirties, I used an electric wheelchair for the first time. I even took it to San Francisco and went racing down the hills.

My wife and I were some of the first people to advocate for ramps so people with disabilities could navigate like everyone else.

When my disease took my voice and I couldn't speak, a computer expert came up with a solution.

And when my hands stopped working and I couldn't even push a button...

Do you think I let that stop me?

In addition to being a scientist, one of my biggest dreams was to write a book that would be fun to read and would explain the universe to millions of people.

A Brief History of Time made me one of the most famous people on the planet.

But a very important result of my newfound fame was raising awareness of my disease and helping other people with disabilities.

In my life, people saw someone who was odd,
who was different,
who was disabled.
But they didn't see me.
I am more than my wheelchair.
I am more than my robotic voice.
I am more than my disability.
Do not let anyone limit you.

As kids, we stare up at the stars with wonder.
We believe that anything is possible.
That should never change.
Life can bring hardship, but it can also bring hope.
Stay curious and keep rolling forward.
When you do...

Using my mind, I have been to the farthest reaches of our galaxy, into a black hole, and back to the beginning of time.

I have been through highs and lows, success and suffering.

I have been able-bodied and disabled.

I have been praised and criticized.

But I have never been ignored.

We are all time travelers, on a journey to the future.
Let us work together to make that future a place we want to visit.
Be brave.
Be curious.
Be determined.
Overcome the odds.
It can be done.

I am Stephen Hawking.
Defy boundaries.

"Black holes... are not the eternal prisons they were once thought.... So, if you feel you are in a black hole, don't give up—there's a way out."
—STEPHEN HAWKING

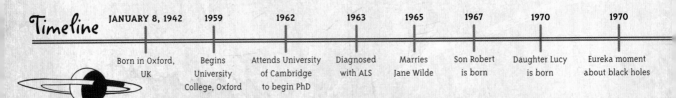

Timeline

JANUARY 8, 1942	1959	1962	1963	1965	1967	1970	1970
Born in Oxford, UK	Begins University College, Oxford	Attends University of Cambridge to begin PhD	Diagnosed with ALS	Marries Jane Wilde	Son Robert is born	Daughter Lucy is born	Eureka moment about black holes

Stephen at age 4

Stephen and wife Jane

Stephen experiences
zero gravity aboard
G-FORCE ONE in 2007

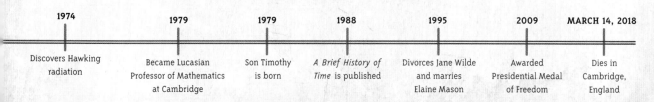

1974	1979	1979	1988	1995	2009	MARCH 14, 2018
Discovers Hawking radiation	Became Lucasian Professor of Mathematics at Cambridge	Son Timothy is born	*A Brief History of Time* is published	Divorces Jane Wilde and marries Elaine Mason	Awarded Presidential Medal of Freedom	Dies in Cambridge, England

In memory of Christopher Reeve,
who I still believe can fly
—B.M.

For Rus Wooton,
a supremely talented artist
who makes the world a better place
for having him in it
—C.E.

For historical accuracy, we used Stephen Hawking's actual words whenever possible. For more of his true voice, we recommend the below titles. Special thanks to Kitty Ferguson for her input on early drafts.

....

SOURCES

My Brief History by Stephen Hawking (Bantam Books, 2013)

A Brief History of Time by Stephen Hawking (Bantam Books, 2017; originally published 1988)

Brief Answers to the Big Questions by Stephen Hawking (Bantam Books, 2018)

Stephen Hawking: A Life Well Lived by Kitty Ferguson (Black Swan, 2019)

A Reader's Companion to Stephen Hawking's A Brief History of Time edited by Stephen Hawking and Gene Stone (Bantam Books, 1992)

A Brief History of Time documentary film directed by Errol Morris (1991)

Hawking documentary film directed by Stephen Finnigan (2013)

FURTHER READING FOR KIDS

Who Was Stephen Hawking? by Jim Gigliotti (Penguin Workshop, 2019)

George's Secret Key to the Universe by Lucy & Stephen Hawking (Simon & Schuster, 2009)

I am Marie Curie by Brad Meltzer and Christopher Eliopoulos (Rocky Pond, 2019)

I am Albert Einstein by Brad Meltzer and Christopher Eliopoulos (Rocky Pond, 2014)

....

ROCKY POND BOOKS
An imprint of Penguin Random House LLC, New York

First published in the United States of America by Rocky Pond Books, an imprint of Penguin Random House LLC, 2024

Text copyright © 2024 by Forty-four Steps, Inc.
Illustrations copyright © 2024 by Christopher Eliopoulos • Coloring by K.J. Díaz with Christopher Eliopoulos

Penguin supports copyright. Copyright fuels creativity, encourages diverse voices, promotes free speech, and creates a vibrant culture.
Thank you for buying an authorized edition of this book and for complying with copyright laws by not reproducing, scanning, or distributing any part of it in any form
without permission. You are supporting writers and allowing Penguin to continue to publish books for every reader.

Rocky Pond Books is a registered trademark and the colophon is a trademark of Penguin Random House LLC.
The Penguin colophon is a registered trademark of Penguin Books Limited.

Visit us online at PenguinRandomHouse.com.

Library of Congress Cataloging-in-Publication Data is available.

Photo on page 38 by Jason Bye; photo of Stephen as a child courtesy of Alamy; photo of Stephen and Jane courtesy of Getty; Zero-G photo courtesy of NASA Image Collection/Alamy

Manufactured in China • ISBN 9780593533390 • 10 9 8 7 6 5 4 3 2 1

TOPL

Design by Jason Henry • Text set in Triplex • The artwork for this book was created digitally.